MW01078065

American
Semi
Trucks

A Photo History of Trucks at Work
1943-1979

Ron Adams

Enthusiast Books

Enthusiast Books

www.enthusiastbooks.com

© 2018 Ron Adams

All rights reserved. No part of this work may be reproduced or used in any form by any means. . . graphic, electronic, or mechanical, including photocopying, recording, taping, or any other information storage and retrieval system. . . without written permission of the publisher.

The information in this book is true and complete to the best of our knowledge. All recommendations are made without any guarantee on the part of the author or Publisher, who also disclaim any liability incurred in connection with the use of this data or specific details.

We acknowledge that certain words, such as model names and designations, mentioned herein are the property of the trademark holder. We use them for purposes of identification only. This is not an official publication.

Enthusiast Books are offered at a discount when sold in quantity for promotional use. Businesses or organizations seeking details should write to the Marketing Department, Enthusiast Books, at the above address.

ISBN-13: 978-1-58388-353-2

Printed in USA

DEDICATION

An accomplishment in one's life is something that the individual can feel very proud of no matter what the accomplishment happens to be: people like Herman "Babe" Ruth, Hank Aaron, Willie Mays, Lou Gehrig, Mickey Mantle, in the field of sports; Johnny Cash, Hank Williams, Patsy Cline, Bill Anderson, Connie Smith, Conway Twitty, in country music; Elvis Presley, Paul Anka, The Beatles, The Lettermen, Roy Orbison, The Rolling Stones, in rock and roll music; Marilyn Monroe, Bob Hope, Carol Burnett, Roy Rogers, Red Skelton, The Three Stooges, in show business. These are just a few people who have accomplished something in their life that has made them known to the rest of the world. People in all walks of life have done things that make other people remember them. Too often a person accomplishes something that does not mean much to other people, but to the individual, it is a good feeling to know that they did this. Let's take this one person. His name is David Kutz. He followed in the footsteps of his older brother and became a truck driver. David was a graduate of the class of 1965 from Kutztown area high school in Kutztown, PA. As he went through his high school years did he want to be a truck driver, or did it just happen that way? Only David knows. He started his job of going to work everyday driving truck for Deka Batteries in Lyons Station, PA. He drove in all kinds of weather; rain, sleet, snow and heat. He was out there with the rest of them making a living at what he liked doing best. I'm sure that not every trip was a piece of cake, but he got from here to there and back again and he did it safely without error. He did this for over 43 years, using eight tractors and totaled up over 9 million miles of safe driving…. equal to going around the world 360 times. Over the course of those years, he occupied spaces at many different truck stops and devoured standby meals of cheeseburgers and French fries with a soda or a 100 mile cup of hot coffee. Through his years of driving he has seen many old time trucks like LJ Macks, DC-75 Autocars, some Bullnose Kenworths, International "Emeryvilles" along with all the design changes from the regular looking trucks to the modern aero-dynamic rigs. He has seen it all- been there, done that. David and I went through high school and graduated together. It never crossed my mind that he would become a truck driver. Well, he did and has accomplished something that not many truck drivers have. David, for your 43+ years of driving truck and 9 million miles of over-the-road safe driving, you earned it. So here it is, this one is for you.

Ron Adams

INTRODUCTION

Many times over the years I've heard guys talking about those golden years of trucking. What and when were those golden years in trucking? What made those the golden years? Who made those the golden years? Well, I think it's a combination of several things. When you are talking with a group of guys, each one has their own opinion about what made those the golden years. This guy might say the trucks he drove. Another guy may say the good money you could earn. Yet another guy might say it was job security because of all the good trucking companies that existed in those days. It really was not only one thing that made those golden years. It was a combination of all the above. When you hear the drivers telling stories of the trucks they drove, what engine it had in it, the transmissions, the rear ends in the trucks and what the truck had on it. This guy might say that a Mack was the best truck. Another guy may say that an Autocar was the best truck. Another might say there was not a truck better then a Sterling. Each guy had his own opinion. I don't think that one truck was better than the other. If a guy drove only Kenworth trucks, naturally he would say Kenworths were the best trucks. If a guy drove Macks all his life then he will say that Macks were the best trucks. I guess we can say that they all got the job done. Then we have the trucking companies. There were many of them back in those years. A lot of them do not exist today due to deregulation. Some of the companies were Nayaud Freight Lines Inc., Pacific Intermountain Express (PIE), Watson Bros. Transportation Co., Spector Freight System, Easters Express Inc. Associated Transport Co., Johnson Motor Lines, Mason-Dixon Lines, East Texas Motor Freight Lines, International Transport Co., and Trans-Cold Express Inc. just to name a few. The guys had their choice depending upon where they lived. A lot of drivers liked the company they drove for because of how the company treated them and also because of the equipment the company operated. During World War II a lot of drivers got taken away from their driving jobs to serve their country in the military. During the war, only one out of every ten trucks that were manufactured were used commercially, the remaining were put to use in the military. By the time the war was over there was a shortage of trucks and most of what was available was in disrepair from constant use. The demand for new trucks was high. When these men returned from war, many of them returned to their former jobs as truck drivers. Some of those returned to the same company they had left, some returned to a different company. After the war, production on new trucks and new models began. One of those new models was the well- liked LJ Mack. They were only made in a three-axle version. Others that came on the scene were the KB and the "W" Model International along with the "L" series, the 3000 White, the "D" Series Conventional GMC cab-over-engine, known as the Cannonball GMC, were some of the new models of the later forties. Many of the trucking companies in the forties and early fifties did not own their own trucks. Owner/Operators leased their trucks to the companies to make up the fleets. In the fifties, many truck manufacturers introduced a lot of new models, which carried on into the sixties and seventies. Several manufacturers disappeared from the scene like, Brockway, Hayes, Brown, Corbitt, and Sterling, to name a few. Also, in the later fifties and sixties, it was the start of the mergers and buy-outs of trucking companies. Examples are Consolidated Freight

Ways getting Motor Cargo; Navajo Freight Lines getting General Expressways; Time Freight getting Super Service Motor Freight; Transcon Lines getting Kramer Bros. Freight Lines; P-I-E getting All states Freight; Interstate Motor Lines getting Eastern Motor Dispatch; just to mention a few. This was beginning of the formation of coast-to-coast carriers. There were more to come, but it would only be a matter of time before a lot of the companies would be paying the price of this thing called "deregulation". When they got into the eighties, many of them packed in in and went out of business. The sad part of it all is that the companies that went out of business are the ones who were the pioneers of the trucking industry. A lot of them were the ones who started trucking back in the twenties and thirties. What surprised a lot of us is that some of the giants left the scene; Transcon Lines, McLean Trucking, P-I-E, Spector, Time-DC, to name a few.

As you look at the pictures in this book you will see some of the things I mentioned like new models of trucks, trucking companies that existed back in the day, some of the different makes and types of trucks and also some of the their beauty. For the newer and younger drivers of today, try to imagine what it would have been like to drive these earlier trucks on the old two lane roads before the new interstate system became a reality. Those old two-lane roads with hills that seemed to take half a day to get to the top in those low-horsepower trucks. Imagine no power steering, no air conditioning, constantly shifting all the time and getting stuck in snowstorms because of the truck's inability to climb the long hills and sitting in a tie-up for hours. This is what it was like back in the day. Yes, they did it and made the best of it and survived. As you look through these pictures and read the captions, I hope you enjoy them as much as I did picking them out to use and writing the captions.

This wartime 1943 Federal is doing double duty with two tandem-axle, dump- trailers. Both trailers dumped from the right side. The power came from a Waukesha, Hercules or Continental Engine. *Combs Photo Service*

Utility Trailer Co. made all kinds of trailers from their beginning in the twenties. The Model SWX-12 trailer is equipped with a Heil Model OT-83-94 hoist and a 16-yard Heil body. The tractor is around a 1946 model 344 Peterbilt. The trailer chassis is a Utility. *Utility Trailers Rode Photo Service*

A mid-1940's White cab-over-engine tractor got selected to pull this unknown brand name reefer trailer. The rig is owned by Wheeler of Menasha, WI. Notice how high the reefer unit is mounted. *Author Collection*

The freshest fruits and vegetables are on their way courtesy of Winn+Lovett's Grocery Co. of Jacksonville, FL with a 1946 C-50-T Autocar on a 156-inch wheelbase. A sleeper cab was ordered for the driver's resting time. The trailer is a 28-foot Miller made in Florida. The Autocars had flat windshields during the forties. *Autocar Trucks*

There are two popular things in this photo. One is the trucking company and the other is the EQ Mack sleeper cab. The company is McLean Trucking of Winston-Salem, NC. The EQ Mack hosts a sleeper cab for sleeper teams running from N. Carolina up the east coast to the middle Atlantic area. The trailer is a Black Diamond. *Author Collection*

Waverly, New York is where this tractor and moving van trailer could be found, No. 1 and No. 1A. The tractor is a 1946 Dodge and the trailer is a Fruehauf. The company is Henson Modern Movers. They did both local and long distance moving. *Author Collection*

Here we have a DC-10064 Autocar with a 171-inch wheelbase. The trailer is an open-top Fruehauf. The company is Costa Distributing Co. based in California. The year is 1946. *Autocar Trucks*

This time we have a 1947-era Dodge pulling a set of Michigan-type flatbed trailers for hauling steel. The owner was T+O Consolidated Freight Co. The white bumber and grille guard give the tractor a little fancy appearance. Take notice that this Dodge looks like it is diesel powered. *Neil Sherff*

The year is 1947. This was the first year for the LT series Mack. The first LT rolled off the line in November 1947. The trailer is a Fruehauf. The rig is owned by California based Balser Truck Co. The way to tell the forties LT from the fifties LT is the forties had the louvers on the side of the hood. The fifties LT had the bulldog and chrome bars. *Mack Trucks*

Here comes a load of thirst quenchers for the city of Sacramento, California. The Regal Pale Distributing Co. of the same city is using a C-100-T Autocar on a 178-inch wheelbase. The tractor is powered by a Hall-Scott engine. The trailer is a Reliance. *Autocar Trucks*

This 1947 Cummins-powered 910 Diamond T belonged to an owner/operator who was leased on with Safeway Truck Lines Inc. of Chicago, Illinois. The trailer is a Brown. Safeway hauled meat, food and food products from the midwest to the east coast and New England. *Joe Wanchura*

The Convoy Company of Portland, Oregon had a wide variety of different types and makes of car haulers. This is a 1947 Ford that was capable of hauling seven cars. The cars on the load are Nash's. *Convoy Company*

Truck-trailer combinations like this were very popular in the western states. This truck is a Kenworth with a livestock body and pull-trailer. Bodies could be Reliance or Merritts. Notice all the round holes in the bumber. This was probably to help cool the engine. The hauler is unknown. *Kenworth Truck Co.*

Here we have another truck-trailer combination. This one is the W-Series International known as the West Coaster model made in Emeryville, California. This all-red, diesel-powered rig was owned by the Dairy Cooperative Association of Portland, Oregon. Both body and trailer were made by Fruehauf. *Photo Art Studio*

The Rock Bros. Co. of New York City, New York used this 1947 Reo for over-the-road hauling. It is pulling a Kingham trailer. It was taking a break in Chicago and posing nicely for the picture. *Joe Wanchura*

Another Chicago picture is this long-hood, 900 Series GMC. The 900 Series had the three small vent doors on the side of the hood. The trailer is a Fruehauf reefer west coast model. The reefer unit is a Thermo-King. The company name is unknown. *Joe Wanchura*

Another Chicago shot is this KB-12 International, diesel-powered. An add-on sleeper box was added for the sleepy driver after a long distance run. The trailer is a Brown reefer. Notice that tractor 143 to the right has the driver sitting in the cab with a flat tire. *Joe Wanchura*

The later forties saw the introduction of White's new cab-over-engine. This is the model 3020T. Many companies used this model because of the short wheelbase and easy maneuvering. This one is hooked up to a Fruehauf moving van trailer for Muller Bros. Moving and Storage of Forest Hills, New York. *White Motor Co.*

Again we have another Chicago shot. This one is a GMC cab-over-engine with a sleeper cab. The tractor is for Zurcher Truck Line of Cozad, Nebraska and is pulling a Brown reefer trailer for Denver Fast Freight. *Joe Wanchura*

Another truck-trailer combination is this model 344 Peterbilt with a flat body and pull trailer. The load looks like it could be plywood. Take notice of where the spare tire is, on top of the load. The haulers name is unknown. *Author Collection*

Another truck-trailer rig. This time it is a tanker unit. The truck is a W-Series International Western Model. Both the wide cab and narrow cab were offered. In this case, the narrow HFW cab was ordered. This is the cab that was made at the International Fort Wayne, Indiana plant. Cummins and Hall-Scott engines were offered. The tank body and trailer were made by Beall Pipe+Tank Corp. in Oregon. Trucking company is unknown. *Beall Inc.*

This set of double trailer operations is a little different than the usual doubles. Most of the double trailers of this era were around 20 to 26 feet long in matching sizes. These trailers were probably used for hauling some kind of fruit or produce. Notice the small vent on the corner of the first trailer. The Cummins powered tractor could be a WC 28 White. *Author Collection*

Here we have another White, which is a WB 22 with a sleeper cab. It is pulling a Fruehauf moving van trailer that is owned by William P. Haley "3A Movers- Anything, Anywhere, Anytime" movers from Portland, Maine. A license plate for every state travelled in was part of the dress code at the time. *Author Collection*

This rig looks a little bit odd because of the short trailer. The tractor is a "C" Model Autocar pulling a 14 to 16 foot dump trailer. Arthur S. Pierce was the owner and hauler. *Autocar Trucks*

This later forties Available truck and trailer tanker outfit was used as a milk hauler. Hawthorn-Mellody Farms of Chicago, Illinois was the rig's owner. The body and trailer brand name are unknown. Notice that the fenders look a lot like the Perterbilt fenders of the time. Available trucks were made in Chicago. *Author Collection*

A lot of the lower numbers in the International "K" Series were gas powered. This after-market job shows that this tractor is powered by a Cummins diesel. This is a rather unique way of mounting the stack. The trailer is a Fruehauf. Notice the boardwalk on top of the cab. The roof of the cab is canvas covered. *Joe Wanchura*

It's evident that when this photo was taken in 1948, Chicago had snow. This DC-100 Autocar braved the cold and snowy conditions that Chicago got. The tractor was employed by Spector Motor Service of Chicago, Illinois running from the Midwest to the East Coast and New England. *Joe Wanchura*

Another truck that was found in Chicago was this GMC tractor that was pulling a Highway reefer trailer. The reefer unit is a Thermo-King. Krey Packing Co. of St. Louis, Missouri is the owner. The power source was probably a 4-banger GMC diesel engine. Notice the Ford sleeper tractor on the left side of the GMC rig. *Joe Wanchura*

This 1949 Freightliner is barreling down the highway with a load of freight headed for parts unknown. This typical western truck-trailer outfit is owned by Vince Graziano. There is probably a sleeper compartment built in the body behind the cab. Notice that the air horn is mounted across the back end of the cab instead of front to back like most of them are. *Freightliner Corp.*

Calhoun Bros. from either Arizona or California, ran this Kenworth Model 523 as a livestock truck-trailer combination. It was powered by a Hall-Scott butane engine. *Kenworth Truck Co.*

A long wheelbase, long nose 900 Series GMC is on duty for Pacific Produce Co. based in California. The unknown make produce-trailer comes equipped with the putt putt motor. The driver stands proud beside the rig. He takes pride in driving. *Author Collection*

Another long-wheelbase western rig is this Model 354 Peterbilt. The rig is owned by Lacy Trucking Co. of Long Beach, California. Their hauling operations were in the oilfields of southern California. Oilfield equipment was their specialty. All the chains and cables that are needed for the job are with the truck, as can be seen. Notice the chrome breather and radiator shell. A little unusual for oilfield rigging. *The Inman Co.*

Not many Corbitts were based in California. However, this one belonged to the Randy Jordan Co. of Los Angeles, California. It had a slightly oversized add-on sleeper box. A reefer trailer followed behind hauling its cargo of refrigerated products. *Author Collection*

One of the biggest trucking companies of the time was Associated Transport Co. Inc. of New York City, New York. The tractor is a Brown and also the trailer. Associated Transport Co. owned both the tractor and trailer manufacturing operations in Henderson, North Carolina. Associated covered the area from the Carolinas up into the middle Atlantic and New England states. The picture was taken in Aberdeen, Maryland in 1952. *Joe Wanchura*

Here we have a somewhat rare Dart tractor with the icicles hanging on the fender, the driver probably just came in from his run for Chicago-Kansas City (C-KC) Freight Lines of Kansas City, Missouri. Dart trucks were made in Kansas City but were later taken over by the Kenworth Motor Truck Co. of Seattle, Washington and then they became known as KW-Dart. *Joe Wanchura*

This brand new 1949 EQT Mack poses for this photo with its partners, a Fruehauf trailer. The rig is owned by Adolphus Rice Mills Inc. of both Houston and Bay City, Texas. A sleeper cab was ordered for the driver to rest in on long overnight runs. *Mack Trucks Inc.*

The load on this Model T-7732 Black Diamond trailer consists of 20 rolls of newsprint. The load is being pulled by a Brockway tractor. The hauler was Paper Board Trucking Corp. of Clifton, New Jersey. *Black Diamond Trailer Co.*

Again, truck-trailer combinations were popular the western states. One company that used some was West Coast Fast Freight Co. of Seattle, Washington. They hauled freight up and down the west coast from Washington and Oregon to California. The truck is a Kenworth. Truck body and trailer brand names are unknown. Notice that in the front of the truck body is a sleeper compartment. West Coast was eventually taken over by Pacific Intermountain Express Co. (P.I.E.) of Oakland, California in 1955. *Author Collection*

The L Model Macks were a very popular series in Mack's line of models. This one happens to be an LJ Mack teamed up with a dump-trailer that is fully loaded with New England Coke. The hauler is C.E. Hall & Sons Inc., Location unknown. Don't take those right turns too fast or you will lose some of your load. *Mack Trucks Inc.*

Tractors with factory sleeper cab were a pretty popular item back in the days. This one happens to be a Model WC-28 White that is powered by a Cummins diesel. The trailer on behind is used for hauling produce. Vent doors and the putt putt motor tell the story. The truck ran out of Oklahoma. *White Motor Co.*

Oilfield work required some big time equipment to haul the big heavy cumbersome machinery. In this case, a 1949 DC 10064 Autocar was chosen to move this piece of machinery on its 266.5 inch wheelbase. A lot of long-wheelbase truck and tractors were used in oilfield hauling. *Autocar Trucks*

Sterling trucks were used in almost every type of hauling in the industry. This Sterling tractor is hooked to a van-trailer. The rig is owned by Robertson Freight Lines. It looks like he is there to pick up a load of Nalley's products. *Author Collection*

This one shows another Sterling but this time as a dump truck. Pazzano Trucking in Massachusetts provided the hauling service for whatever the load was. Waukesha, Cummins and Buda diesel engines were available as power sources. *Ken Hird Photo*

Well, it snowed again in Chicago. This time we have a Corbitt tractor that is pulling a Dorsey trailer. Owner and the Company are unknown. The power comes from either a Continental, Hercules, or a Cummins engine. *Joe Wanchura*

This Freightliner was owned by Consolidated Freightways Inc. of Portland, Oregon. On the door it shows Chicago and the license plate shows Illinois 1949. The rig was most likely based at their Chicago terminal and ran the Upper Midwestern states. Notice how close the nose of the trailer is to the back of the cab. The overall length was shortened to make it within the legal length limit in the Midwest states. *Joe Wanchura*

The question here is are these two trailers being loaded on to or are they being unloaded from the railroad car. Whatever the case may be, the job is being done by a "C" Model Autocar tractor that is owned by the Pacific Motor Trucking Co. which is the trucking division of the Southern Pacific Railroad. Notice on the number that there is a pin hookup. The reason for this was so that the tractor could be used to back trailers up to the docks when a dolly was hooked to the trailer. *Author Collection*

A popular truck of this era was the White. This WC-22 PHT is one of many that ran on our highways back in the days. The trailer is a half and half. The front half is closed top and the back half is open top. The rig is privately owned by Arrow Engineering Co. of Mooresville, Indiana. Notice the two vent doors on the front of the trailer. *White Motor Co.*

Double trailers was another type of combination ran out west. These are two milk tanker-trailers that are being pulled by a Kenworth tractor. The Carnation Co. claims ownership of the rig. The company colors were red. *Author Collection*

One of the bigger western companies was Illinois-California Express with their home office in Denver, Colorado. They had a variety of different makes of trucks and trailers in their fleet. An example of that is this 1949-50 Kenworth and a much newer Brown trailer. These conventional tractors were used west of Denver. Before the name ICX existed, the name was Los Angeles-Albuquerque Express. Notice the spare tire rack behind the sleeper box. Also notice from the previous photos that the big west coast mirrors are now being seen on all trucks. The previous one were small round one or small rectangular ones. *Author Collection*

By this time, 1950, Freightliner was selling trucks to commercial users. Three of those trucks were sold to the Hyster Co. in Portland, Oregon. to haul tractor equipment and tools. Peerless trailers are carrying the loads. *Author Collection*

1949 was the first year that Peterbilt started making cab-over-engine trucks. The one new model was this 360 model. According to the records, only 14 were made from 1949 to 1952. The one seen here is from King Beef used to haul livestock one way and freight the other way with this truck-trailer combination. *Author Collection*

Another truck-trailer outfit like this one was used by a number of carriers in the Northwest in freight and tankers. In this case Lee+Easter Inc. of Seattle, Washington shows us one of their freight outfits, which also had a tanker division. The body is mounted on a Freightliner truck. Notice the long fuel tank. *Author Collection*

Still another Freightliner on a long wheelbase chase. No company name is known. The trailer is a bottom unload tank but no brand name either. Notice the steps and railing to get to the top of the tank. *Author Collection*

Still another truck-trailer combination is this tanker outfit. The 1950 tractor is a big 900 Series GMC diesel. It is owned by the Western Condensing Co., Location unknown. Notice the small rectangle mirrors. *Author Collection*

This Brown tractor does not have too much to tell us. Associated Transport Co. ran Brown sleepers like this one but here it is in someone else's ownership. Notice who is standing tall of the radiator shell. *Joe Wanchura*

Here we have a Model 350 Peterbilt cab-over-engine. It is owned by Belyea Truck Co.,based in California. On the trailer is loaded a Caterpillar bulldozer. The blade is being pulled behind on a dolly. Notice the sign on the building. It's so nice that everybody obeys the rules. *Author Collection*

A 1951 Corbitt is backed up to the dock waiting to unload. The diesel-powered tractor has a sleeper cab for the drivers resting time. An air conditioner was added to cool the hot days for the driver. The reefer trailer could be a Utility. The rig was hauling for The Daniel Co. *Author Collection*

Here we have another Corbitt, but in the cab-over-engine version. The Corbitt had a high day-cab. It looks like during working time it hauled produce and seafood for some refrigerated line. *Neil Sherff*

Ellis Trucking Co. was a Midwest company that operated around the Indiana area. This Chevrolet tractor and Fruehauf trailer hauled freight around town and over the road. A Huber and Huber Motor Express trailer somehow made its way to the Eillis terminal. *Neil Sherff*

A 1951 F-8 Ford tractor is kept busy hauling freight in the open-top trailer for Associated Truck Lines of Grand Rapids, Michigan. They hauled freight in a five-state area in the Midwest from Chicago to Pittsburgh and in Michigan and Indiana. *Neil Sherff*

Here, there, and everywhere pretty much tells the territory that this 1951 UD-204 Autocar traveled in. Tanners Transfer+ Storage Co. of Richmond, Virginia did the moving. The driver's door on this model opened from the front. It had a very streamlined body. *Autocar Trucks*

Consolidated Freightways of Portland, Oregon was about one of the largest trucking companies in the country. Their over-the-road tractor fleet was made up of almost all White-Freightliner tractors. This Strick trailer had a roll front roof or what was known as a roll-roof trailer. In this photo, caution had to be taken because of the high stack on the tractor. *Author Collection*

One of the bigger tractors of the day was the WC-28 White. This one was teamed up with a Dorsey produce trailer. The rig was owned by Harry Driden Produce of Virginia. Notice Donald Duck on the door. *Neil Sherff*

A DC-100 Autocar has the honors of hauling a load of Acme Beer in this 1940's Fruehauf trailer. Wade Transportation Co. had no problem getting the load to its destination with this Autocar. *Autocar Trucks*

One of the popular carriers that moved freight up and down the east coast was Akers Motor Lines of Gastonia, North Carolina. One of the many tractors that were used was this DC-7513 Autocar that was owned by C.M. Tilley of Charlotte, North Carolina. *Autocar Trucks*

Many of these WC-22 Whites ran the highways back in the day. This one was on with Lightning Express Inc. of Pittsburgh, Pennsylvania. To go with this White was a Fruehauf trailer. Notice the Kilgo Freight Lines trailer that made its way to the terminal probably through interlining. *Lightning Express Inc.*

Another White that was kept busy working is this one that pulled in the steel division for Yellow Transit Freight Lines of Indianapolis, Indiana. The power came from a Cummins diesel. Notice that on the radiator shell is a mirror that is angled towards the stack. This was so the driver could see the fire that came from the stack at night. *Neil Sherff*

Here we have two sets of twins. The first set is two identical Diamond T tractors with sleeper cabs. Both are diesel powered. The second set of twins are the two Great Dane produce-trailers. Both rigs belong to Tart Bros. of Orlando, Florida. *Author Collection*

This Big International West Coaster truck is an L-400. Engines that were offered were Cummins diesels and Hall-Scott 200 HP gas engines. The truck is owned by Eastern Washington Transport. Notice the small rectangular mirrors and also the fire extinguisher for just in case. *Author Collection*

In 1951 Reo changed their grille style by putting the letter R-E-O down the middle and added two chrome bars. Republic Van Lines of Los Angeles, California used this Reo that was powered by Reo's Gold Comet engine to pull the Utility moving van trailer. The company had an add-on sleeper box for the driver on his cross-country runs. *Author Collection*

A workhorse of a truck was this model LM Mack. Chase Transfer Corp. put the truck to the test by using it to haul this heavy load. Chase was located in Portland, Maine. A Jo-Dog was used because of the extra weight. *Author Collection*

The W-71 Mack started production in 1953 to 1958. The production count was 215. One of those was this one owned by ORE-IDA Potato Products Inc. of Ontario, Oregon. That is hooked up to a reefer trailer probably loaded with potato products. Mack made the W-71 in a day cab only. Sleeper cab extensions and box sleepers were after market jobs. *Kent Gilman*

Another Mack cab-over-engine was the H-61, known as the "cherry picker" because of its height. The production time was from 1952 to 1957. The production count on these was 484. Security Van and Storage Co. of Elba, Alabama had this H-61 hooked to a Kingham moving trailer. *Author Collection*

Here we have a mixed fleet of WC-2864 TD's and WC 22T's. This was a joint venture between United Truck Lines, Northern Pacific Transport and Buckingham Transportation Co. through interlining from the Upper Midwest to the Northwest. The "B" on the door tells me that the tractors are owned by Buckingham Transportation Co. of Rapid City, South Dakota. The photo was taken in Billings, Montana. *Author Collection*

Another Pacific coast carrier was Los Angeles-Seattle Motor Express Inc. of Seattle, Washington. L.A.S.M.E. used a wide variety of different makes of trucks and types of rigs. This example is a model 350 Peterbilt cab-over-engine as a truck-trailer combination. Truck body and trailer were made by Trailmobile. Notice the sleeper compartment in the nose of the body. In 1969, L.A.S.M.E. became one of the carriers to form the big time-DC system. *Author Collection*

Peterbilt also had a model 350 conventional truck. The one seen here was known as the "Iron Nose Pete". This is a rather sharp looking Peterbilt for the time. It had more chrome then usual. It was teamed up to a Trailmobile produce-trailer for some unknown carrier. *Author Collection*

This is the new C-750 Ford cab-over-engine for 1953. The big V-8 engine gave it the power to get the job done. Hauling steel and steel products was its job while working for Brada Cartage Co. of Kokomo, Indiana. Nothing fancy, just a good ol' plain Jane tractor. *Neil Sherff*

Another model from Mack was the "A" series. This one is a 1953 era. It's hooked to a Strick trailer for Shein's Express. Notice the small round mirrors that are still being used. *Shein's Express*

The date of delivery on this truck says August 1953. It is a model B-50T Mack with a Charlotte sleeper cab. Could this be the first B-50 that Mack made? The trailer is a Dorsey. Ruberoid is the company who punchased the rig. *The Overbey Studio*

Many of us remember seeing these "Cannonball" GMC diesel trucks running the highways between Colorado and the New England states. They were shown to us by Riss and Company of Kansas City, Missouri hauling lots of meat products and other freight between the Midwest and cities like Boston, Philadelphia, Jersey City, New York City, to mention a few on the east coast. The return loads were sometimes explosives. Back around 1953, Riss ordered a fleet of 500 of them at one time! The trailer is a Strick. *Neil Sherff*

Hostess Cupcakes and Wonder Bread made their way to the distributors in trucks like this truck-trailer combo GMC. The body and trailer were made by Brown trailers. Private carriers also used these kinds of combinations and not only the trucking companies. *Author Collection*

Here we have a 1954 White for Petroleum Carriers Corp. of Minneapolis, Minnesota which was a division of Ruan Transport Co. of Des Moines, Iowa. It looks like gasoline is the liquid commodity being transported in the Fruehauf tank-trailer. Notice the fire extinguisher for a just in case. *White Motor Co.*

Ringsby Truck Lines Inc. was one of the four big carriers based in Denver, Colorado. They ran from the west coast to as far east as Chicago. They had four divisions. One of those four divisions was their reefer division that had operating rights to travel over any routes in the country on Ringsby's irregular route authority. One of those trucks was the bullnose Kenworth pulling what looks like a Utility reefer trailer. Bob Ward tells me that any tractor that had a permanent lease contract with Ringsby Reefer Division had to be painted this two-tone green and white. *Ringsby Reefer Div.*

This mid-fifties, White-Freightliner looks a little strange but out west they experimented and tried anything to get the most hauling space they could. They started by designing a 48-inch pancake cab putting the sleeper on top of the cab. Then they made a Hi-Cube body and trailer using every inch they could to fill in the space and keep it within the legal length. Both body and trailer were made by Utility. The Williamette Valley Company in Eugene, Oregon was the proud owner used to haul building materials. *Joe Wanchura*

The uniformed driver is ready to go and make his run. On this trip he will do it in a DC-10264 Autocar that is powered by a Buda diesel. He will do the run for O.M. Slosson of Long Beach, California. Gasoline is most likely the commodity being hauled in the tank body and trailer. *Author Collection*

Another truck that ran California was this C-10064 Autocar. It pulled a Fruehauf stainless steel trailer for Mueller Truck Co. in San Diego, California. The two road lights below the bumber are located in good positions. The right one shines to show the edge of the road and shoulder and the left one shines to guide with the white line. *Autocar Trucks*

This R Model International of the 1954 era was owned by Eastern Motor Express Inc. of Terre Haute, Indiana. It was one of many in their fleet. The trailer is a Fruehauf with a big box Thermos-King reefer unit. The trailer is owned by Des Moines Transportation of Des Moines, Iowa. This is what was known as interlining. The photo was taken at the Bedford, PA. relay station. *Neil Sherff*

"Sweet Thing" with its under-cover load decided to take a rest break after hours of a long, hard, run. The RDC "High Binder" International is decked out with 5 bullet-cab-lights, dual airhorns, dual stacks, and a nice paint job. This truck was still running yet in 1970. *Harry Patterson*

This real sharp looking 1954 Model 300 GMC is decked out with a fancy chrome grille, dual airhorns, 5 cab-lights, and big west coast mirrors to make you say "wow". The livestock body was made by Beco Bodies. The owner of the truck is probably the gentle-men standing beside the truck, Fred Chambers of Knoxville, Iowa. *GMC Trucks*

The Model 350 "Iron Nose" Peterbilt poses proudly to have its picture taken after having its new tank body and trailer installed. The body and trailer were made by Industrial Steel Tank and Body Co. We don't know who the truck owner was, but we know that it is truck number 531. *Industrial Steel + Body*

The previous photo was a 350 Peterbilt. This tractor is also a 350 Peterbilt but of the cab-over-engine version. The rig is owned by Jack Maus of Minnesota. It is pulling an unknown brand reefer trailer. They stood tall, didn't they? *Harry Patterson*

Brockway trucks were a popular truck in the New England and middle Atlantic area. This sleeper cab version is owned by T+T Trucking of Little Falls, New York. It's pulling an unusual type of Fruehauf stainless steel trailer. Take note that it is still using the small round mirrors yet. *Brockway Trucks*

This C-8564 Autocar is on duty as a concrete mixer truck. It travels on a 176- inch wheelbase and rides on 10:00x22 tires. The power comes from a Mustang 390A engine. The mixer body is a Rex Adjusta-Wate 6 1/2 yard; 9-yard agitator capacity. It is kept busy by Trans Materials Co. of Berwyn, Pennsylvania. *Autocar Trucks*

The Model-3000 White was introduced around 1949-1950. This one is around 1955 and it is owned by Cook Truck Lines of Memphis, Tennessee. It is hooked up to a Fruehauf volume van-trailer with a sliding tandem. *Author Collection*

Another large carrier that was based in Denver, Colorado was Navajo Freight Lines Inc. Running from the west coast, through the Southwest, up to Denver and then east to Chicago, they used equipment like this White-Freightliner that was probably used east of Denver because of the length laws. Their trailers were really eye catching when you saw the big Navajo name. The two gentlemen in the picture are unknown but one of them could be Lawrence Cohen. The photo was taken at the home office in Denver. *Navajo Freight Lines Inc.*

Los Angeles-Seattle Motor Express Inc. of Seattle, Washington had a variety of different makes of tractors in their fleet. This Kenworth was one of many that were in their fleet. The Aero-Liner trailer partners very nice with this tractor. Their trucks could be seen running up and down along the pacific coast. *L.A.S.M.E*

Texas Meat and Provision Co. of Dallas, Texas hauled meat and swinging beef coast to coast. One of the tractors that were used to get the job done was this mid-fifties bullnose Kenworth tractor. The Fruehauf stainless reefer trailer carried the goods. The owners and drivers were Joe Spiritas and Archie Sloan. The picture was taken in the Pennsauken, New Jersey area on Sept. 27th 1955. *Robert Parrish*

Two trailers of heavily bagged cement pose no problem for this 521 Kenworth, as it runs through California. Permanent Cement Co. Also ran double bulk cement trailers. *Author Collection*

Don't let that little guy on the radiator cap fool you. The truck is not a Mack, it is a Kenworth. He is only going along for a ride. This truck-trailer combination is owned by the American Oil Co.. Dual stacks, dual air horns, air conditioner, and grille guard are unusual items for a company truck. The rig shows a Montana license plate. *Author Collection*

Southern Pacific Truck Service was the trucking division of the Southern Pacific Railroad. The tractor is a DC-405 International. This short-wheelbase tractor could pull two 24-foot trailers and have the legal length of 60 feet. *S.P. Truck Service*

It is too bad that we can't see this truck in color. The colors of this LT Mack and trailer were painted black and bright green. Catching the eye are dual chrome stacks, dual air horns, chrome radiator shell plus more that make this one nice-looking truck. No wonder the driver has a smile on his face. The truck is owned by Bardahl of So. California, based 7565 Melrose Ave. in Los Angeles. *Author Collection*

At this time Daniels Motor Freight Inc. of Warren, Ohio had over 400 trucks operating in their fleet. A lot of them were owner-operators. This owner was M.W. Weigle and ran down the road with this REO tractor that was powered by Reo's popular Gold Comet engine. Tagging on behind is a Dorsey trailer. "The Flying Cloud" could be seen running the highways between Chicago and the east coast. *Neil Sherff*

Many produce and reefer haulers ran from the southern states up the east coast and to the Midwest. One of those companies was Alterman Transport Lines of Miami, Florida. The tractor is an H63 Mack. Tagging on behind is a Great Dane reefer trailer. Great Dane trailers were very popular with the southern haulers. Notice the boardwalk on the top of the cab. This was used so that the driver could check the reefer bit without standing on the cab roof. *Author Collection*

From the Gulf to the Great Lakes was the hauling territory of East Texas Motor Freight Lines Inc. of Dallas, Texas. The tractors are White 9000 TD's. The trailers, from left to right, are Fruehauf, Trailmobile, Strick and Andrews. The picture was taken at the Dallas coliseum. *Ed Miley Photographic*

A truckload of Sparkletts drinking water is on the way to quench the thirst of the California residents. A GMC tractor pulls the load on double trailers. I'm estimating that there are 408 bottles on this load. Both trailers are Fruehaufs. *Author Collection*

Truck-trailer combinations were seen in the western states. The body is mounted of the chassis of a White 302464. The owner and the brand name of the truck body and trailer are unknown. *White Motor Co.*

This 1956 White-Freightliner is ready to roll with two Trailmobile trailers. The sleeper team is ready to start their run to somewhere within the Ringsby system, probably leaving Denver. The names of the sleeper team drivers are unknown. *Ringsby Truck Lines Inc.*

Here we have a Kenworth CBE (cab-beside-engine) sleeper. This model was introduced around 1954. The trailer is a Brown. The rig is owned by Illinois-California Express (I-C-X) of Denver, Colorado. Their routes were from California through the southwest and up to Denver and then east into Chicago. *Author Collection*

Pacific Intermountain Express (P.I.E.) of Oakland, California covered the western states east to Denver and then east to St.Louis and Chicago. Their operation consisted of several divisions. One of those divisions was a tanker operation. In that division they had tractor-trailers, double trailers and truck-trailers such as the one shown here. This is about a1956-57 Kenworth. These types of rigs did not go east of Denver due to the length laws. *P.I.E.*

Kenworth trucks were pretty popular for that extra fancy look. It's not too fancy compared to today's trucks, but back in its time, it got plenty of looks. The dual chrome stacks, air horns, chrome breaker, bullet lights and few extra pieces made owner Tony Beovich of Portland, Oregon feel proud to run down the highway in his rig pulling the Trailmobile reefer trailer. *Author collection*

Trucks for Watson Bros. Transportation Co. Inc. of Omaha, Nebraska could be seen from California to Chicago and points in between. The truck is seen in Nebraska. It is a DC-405 International pulling a Fruehauf trailer. Watson Bros was one of the largest companies at the time. *A.T.H.S*

This C-800 Ford of 1956 vintage was working for K+L Beverage Co. of Seattle, Washington. It was hauling the Lucky Lager Brew in this Brown trailer. This design only existed for about two years. *Author Collection*

This is another Ford, but of the "F" Series. This F-800 was as a straight truck and pulled about a 20-foot trailer behind. The rig is leased on with Brada Cartage Co. of Kokomo, Indiana. It looks like this "big job" Ford has no problem hauling its load of steel coils. *Neil Sherff*

The two hand shakers joined the north and south through Mason and Dixon Lines of Kingsport, Tennessee. At this time Mason and Dixon covered from Chicago south to Tennessee and up north to the middle Atlantic states. The hauling was done with trucks like this B-61 Mack partnered with a Brown trailer. *Author Collection*

Another Mack is this 1956 B-70 Model. It was owned by the Shell Oil Company in California pulling a gasoline tank-trailer of yellow and red that was made by Weld Build Trailer CO. *Author Collection*

The second or the third largest trucking company in the mid-fifties was Roadway Express Inc. of Akron, Ohio. Roadway was started by two brothers, Carroll and Galen Rouch back in 1930. By 1956 Roadway served almost every state east of the Mississippi river and a few states west of it. Roadway ran a lot of sleeper teams using trucks like this H-63 Mack and Gindy trailer. *Neil Sherff*

An east coast, north and south carrier was Pilot Freight Carriers of Winston-Salem, North Carolina. This 921-C Diamond T tractor and COPCO trailer was one of the many outfits that transported freight over the Pilot routes. This cab had the Busel back sleeper. *Pilot Freight Carriers*

This W-71 Mack was kept busy hauling livestock over the western roads. There is no name to tell who owns the rig. A lot of livestock haulers in the West used combinations like this one. The make of the body and the trailer are also unknown. Photo was taken in Fresno, California. *Joe Wanchura*

The B-73 was a tractor designed for the western trucker. Here we have a B-73 that is hooked to a set of double-bottom-dump, gravel-trailers. California based Consolidated Rock Co. is the owner. The tractor was powered by a Cummins diesel. *Author Collection*

Dromedary's were also a western type operation. The one pictured here was used by Pacific Intermountain Express (P.I.E.) of Oakland, California. Because of the length, these ran only west of Denver and into California. The twin-steer tractor is a Kenworth with a Brown drom body and a Strick trailer. The engine is mounted on its side. *P.I.E.*

The very popular "cannonball" GMC found their place in the fleets of many trucking companies. This Model 860 does not show who the owner is, but we see that it is pulling a Traillmobile reefer trailer for Cargo-Sure Polar Stream. The tractor has a few added extras to give it the custom look. *Stan Holtzman*

Another GMC is this Model-860. This was the 1957-era pulling a reefer trailer. The company it leased on with was Trans-Cold Express Inc. of Dallas, Texas. An add-on box sleeper was there for the drivers resting time. Trans-Cold Express Inc. ran nationwide hauling meat and swinging beef out of Texas. *Neil Sherff*

Another GMC was this smaller 500 Series tractor. Cross-country driving made the driver tired so a sleeper box was added. The trailer is a Utility moving-van trailer. The truck was hauling for Bekins Van Lines of Omaha, Nebraska. *Robert Parrish*

Another popular fleet tractor was this Model 9000 White. The tractor was not only popular but these Fruehauf volume van trailers were also popular with a lot of carriers. In this case the interested customer was Indianapolis-Kansas City Motor Express (I.K.C) of Indianapolis, Indiana. A Cummins Diesel was the power source for this rig. *I.K.C. Motor Express*

This great looking DC-10064 Autocar with the Fruehauf body and trailer following on behind for the Keil Grocery Co. of Billings, Montana got attention as it travelled down the western highways. The dual chrome stacks and the four road-lights, which I like, are eye catching. *Autocar Trucks*

This time our attention is on this DC-75 Autocar. It is powered by a 220 Cummins diesel? A Great Dane produce-trailer follows on behind. John Baggett Transportation is the rig's owner. *Neil Sherff*

Here we see the first cab-over-engine tractor that Reo made. This was in 1956. It was in the fleet of Brada Cartage Co. in Kokomo, Indiana hauling steel products. *Neil Sherff*

This Diamond T cab-over-engine could be mistaken for an International since it is an International cab. The trailer is a Dorsey. Chun-King of Duluth, Minnesota kept the rig bust hauling Chun-King Oriental Foods. *Diamond Truck Co.*

This Model 281 Peterbilt tractor was pulling double-bulk, pneumatic tanker-trailers for Ray Sharp Trucking of Long Beach, California. Although it is a single axle tractor, the wheelbases varied. The trailers are Utility. *Author Collection*

This Model 351 cab-over-engine Peterbilt was made up as a dromedary rig. The body was a Brown, but trailer was unknown. It was designed for hauling lite-weight freight. Notice the doors in the front of the trailer. This was probably designed to load the Drom body by backing the rig up the dock and then loading the trailer and then into the body. You could say that this was the volume hauler for lite-weight freight. The owner of the truck and its location are unknown. Most likely a California based rig. *Author Collection*

Back in the day while traveling our American highways, you could see these yellow and green trucks on the same highways hauling all different kinds of loads. This load is a load of tow motor forklifts. The company hauling the load is International Transport Inc. of Rochester, Minnesota who was a heavy hall carrier. The tractor, number 102, is a late fifties DCOT-405 International, known as the Emeryville. The trailer has an undercount rack for the open rack side kit. Of course, part of the dress code of the day was a lot of license plates. *International Transport*

The big brute in this photo is a B-61 Mack with the integral sleeper cab. On behind he is pulling a Great Dane reefer trailer. The company is Grady Sisco Farm Products of East Prairie, Missouri. A little bit of decorating can make a truck look nice. If you wanted to talk to the driver of this truck, his reply would have probably been "Need dough, Must go". I love that trailer high stack. *Neil Sherff*

The new model of the AC line debuted in 1957 and only lasted two years before the new BC line was introduced. The one we see here is and AC-225 in a sleeper cab version. The power came from a Cummins diesel with several choices of horsepower. The trailer is a Dorsey reefer. The trucking company was based in Florida. *Author Collection*

McLean Trucking Co. of WInston-Salem, North Carolina was one of several big southern trucking companies that ran from the southern states up the Atlantic coast to the middle Atlantic and New England states. One of the rigs used was this Model 860 "cannonball" GMC and Trailmobile open-top trailer. GMC tractors seemed to dominate the fleet. *McLean Trucking Co.*

What may look like a 9000 White is actually a 4000 Model White. The difference between the two is that the 4000 Model has the long hood and the 9000 model has the short hood. Dual chrome stacks and a sleeper box that says it's a Transicold Box, that I rather doubt, were added extras. It was leased on with the Refrigerated Food Express in Boston, Mass. *Neil Sherff*

Another refrigerated hauler was Frigid Meats Inc. of Chicago, Illinois. The rig we see here is a DC-7564 Autocar tractor pulling a Fruehauf reefer trailer. Again, we see dual stack, dual air horns and a sleeper box. The advertising on the trailer lets the public know who you are. *Neil Sherff*

This California set of double flatbed-trailers was used for hay hauling. The tractor used for pulling the set is a DCO-405 International "Emeryville". I cannot make out the name, but the rig is California based. *Stan Holtzman*

A Chevrolet 50 Viking tractor and a Model 300 40-foot Utility-van trailer are teamed together on April 23, 1958 for their show time picture. The owner is Accurate Corrugated Specialty Corp. of Los Angeles, California; manufacturers of quality shipping containers. *Utility Trailer Co.*

Reefer hauling in the middle part of the country was a popular haul in the later fifties with each refrigerated carrier having their share of the cold freight. One of those carriers was Little Audreys Transportation Co. in Fremont, Nebraska which later became part of the Midwest's Emery Freight System Inc. in Chicago, Illinois. A lot of Little Audrey's runs were made to the west coast. One of those trucks could have been this 921-C Diamond T with the Bussel back sleeper cab and pulling a Fruehauf reefer trailer. Little Audrey's colors were blue + Grey. *Neil Sherff*

Pacific Intermountain Express (P.I.E.) of Oakland, California always took nice photographs of their equipment. This photo is no exception. Here they show us a 351 Peterbilt with a sleeper box pulling a Trailmobile van trailer. The length laws kept this type of equipment from running east of Denver. *P.I.E.*

E.A. Miller Farm Produce of McMinnville, Tennessee had this 921F Diamond T sleeper and Dorsey reefer trailer hauling their products to eastern markets. Notice the safety precaution the driver took by putting a block of wood in front of the tractor tandem to keep the rig from moving forward. *Author Collection*

Oranges, oranges, and more oranges are being hauled in this set of Fruehauf bulk-trailers. The tractor pulling the set of doubles is a 281 Peterbilt. This is how the oranges came in from the orchard to the cannery. Sunkist growers in California was the orchard. *Author Collection*

The H-67 was the next model in the line after the H-63 in the Mack line-up. K.C. Bernard of Ft.Worth, Texas is the owner of the rig, but it is leased to Samuels and Co. of Dallas, Texas. The trailer is an early fifties Hobbs reefer. *Neil Sherff*

North American Van Lines in Fort Wayne, Indiana was about the largest household goods mover in the country. One of the rigs among the fleet was this Model 260 Brockway sleeper with a Dorsey moving-van trailer. Their colors were maroon, cream and black. This gas job probably has a Brockway Continental engine. *Author Collection*

U.S. Truck Company of Detroit, Michigan ran a large fleet of steel hauling rigs in Michigan and Ohio. The wheel and trailer configuration varied somewhat but the one shown here is a 2-2-2-2-1 axle setup. The tractor is a B-80 Mack pulling two Michigan-type flatbed, steel-trailers. This rig is in the steel division. *Neil Sherff*

One of the older trucking companies that got their start back in 1932 was Continental Transportation Lines Inc. of Pittsburgh, Pennsylvania. Over the years Continental, like many carriers, used a variety of different brand makes of truck and trailers. In the late-fifties they were using Model 9000 Whites and Strick trailers like the one shown here. The states they served were Ohio, Pennsylvania, New Jersey, New York and Maryland. The tractor is powered by a 195-HP Cummins diesel with a 10-speed transmission. *Continental Transportaion Lines Inc.*

During the 1950's Transcon Lines of Oklahoma City, Oklahoma ran from the Pacific cost through the Southwest as far east as Chicago and Atlanta, Georgia in the south. This White-Freightliner was one of 300 tractors and the Fruehauf trailer was one of 400. The company was founded in 1946. The company made amazing progress in the 14 years of their existence. *Transcon Lines Inc.*

Longer wheelbase tractors were always a nice sight to see. This RDF-400 International west coaster is a good example of that. Dual stacks, dual air horns and sun visor add a little extra to the appearance. The trailer on the back is used for hauling grain. Bennett and White of Greeley, Colorado are the owners. *Author Collection*

Earlier we had a photo of a rig for Sunkist on the west coast. Now we go across country to the east coast. Tropicana products of Bradenton, Florida used this model 9000 White to pull the Fontaine tank-trailer that was used for hauling citrus pulp. It looks like a very high trailer. *Lamar Philpot Photography*

Another household goods carrier was Allied Van Lines Inc. of Broadview, Illinois. To move the goods they used this C-600 Series Ford and Fruehauf moving van trailer. Their trucks wore the company colors of orange and black. The dual stacks, that probably made a lot of noise, made the truck a little more tough. The agent was Potter Moving + Storage Co. of Royal Oak, Michigan. *Neil Sherff*

A west coast style tractor was this long wheelbase 921-F Diamond T tractor pulling a Trailmobile van-trailer with a load of Falstaff Beer for the west coast drinkers. The wheelbase is stretched out to about 260 inches. *Author Collection*

The southern drivers seemed to like their integral sleepers. This big B-73 Mack sleeper cab looked tough hooked up to the Dorsey produce trailer. The power was provided courtesy of a Cummins diesel. C.E. Swafford Produce and Grain of Cullman, Alabama were the owners. *Neil Sherff*

The mate to the previous B-73 Mack is this G-73 Mack cab-over-engine. The owner is Ralph Rush of Anaheim, California. It was also powered by a Cummins diesel to pull the Lufkin reefer trailer. Production of the "G" Model started in 1959. *Author Collection*

Here we have another G-73 but this time in a single-axle version. The tractor is pulling a Fruehauf van-trailer that is in the fleet of Middle Atlantic Transportation Co. Inc. of Bridgeport, Conn. They covered the area between the Atlantic and out to Michigan. *Neil Sherff*

Here we have another Mack. This time it's a B-75 Model that had the big Mack diesel engine. This sleeper cab was known as the Charlotte sleeper. The B-73 and B-75 Models replaced the LT Series in 1956-57. Check out the trailer high stack. The tractor was owned by Jack Collings of Pompano Beach, Florida. *Neil Sherff*

In the later fifties, double 40-foot trailers were starting to be legal on the thru-ways. This unit is two 35-foot trailers, first one is with two 17-foot containers and the second is a 35-foot trailer. The tractor is a 1959 DCO-405 International "Emeryville" and both trailers are Fruehaufs. The power came from a 335 HP Cummins diesel. This outfit ran the Massachusetts turnpike and the New York state thruway. Its run was from Boston to Ripley, New York. The distance was 540 miles. The company was Spector Freight System of Chicago, Illinois. A two-man team did the driving. *Author Collection*

This H-67 Mack had the job of pulling the Black Diamond Furniture trailer. The rig is owned by the Hickory Chair Co. in Hickory, North Carolina. I guess it is evident as to what the truck is hauling. There were many furniture manufacturers and haulers out of North Carolina. *Author Collection*

Many Michigan carriers were steel haulers or had a steel division in their operation as is the case here. Darling Freight Inc. had this Model 3000 White sleeper and the spread-axle trailer in their steel division that operated in Michigan, Indiana and Ohio. *Neil Sherff*

International's ACO cab-over-engine model is a little different looking than other cab-over–engine models. They were known as the Sightliner. The earlier models had single headlights and the new ones had the duals. The engines offered were a V-401, V-461 or the big V-549. This ACO is equipped with a Dromedary body on the long wheelbase tractor. A good idea to use the extra space for freight hauling because usually you bring home the bread, but in this case the bread is being delivered. I want to make a note of one thing: In the Fredrick Crimson book on International trucks he states that in September 1957 is when International first introduced this new ACO model. How do you explain the 1956 license plate? *Author Collection*

Chevrolet trucks seemed to be a big hit with the household goods carriers. The new 1960 Chevrolet cab-over-engine was owned by Cox-Patrick, who were in business since 1900, and were agents for United Van Lines in Houston, Texas. The trailer is a Fruehauf. Notice all the state permit numbers on the side of the trailer. *Art Meyer Photography*

This DC-9264 Autocar was working for the Ray L. Atchinson Construction Co. in Aztec, New Mexico. It has a 235-inch wheelbase and is powered by a 280 HP turbocharged diesel engine with a 5-speed main and a 4-speed auxiliary transmission and running on 11:00/22 tires. The drop trailer is a Timpte with a Euclid C6 bulldozer on its back. *Autocar Trucks*

Another Autocar is this DC-10264TL tractor with a 199-inch wheelbase. It has the Autocar sleeper cab, a 262-HP diesel engine with a 5-speed main and a 3-speed auxiliary transmission and riding on 10:00-20 tires. The trailer is a Dorsey reefer owned by Kilgore Inc. of Westerville, Ohio. *Autocar Trucks*

This big International is a 220 powered by a Cummins diesel. A sleeper cab was chosen for long runs. It is pulling an Aero-Liner produce trailer. The owner is Anderson Chemical Co. of Litchfield, Minnesota. Notice the little mirror on the top of the hood so the driver can see the fire shooting from the stack at night. *Neil Sherff*

Trans American Freight Lines Inc. had a steel division as did many other carriers. One of the trucks in their steel division was this 5000 White hooked to a flatbed-trailer with a side kit. Trans American was based in Detroit, Michigan. *Neil Sherff*

The White 9000 was owned by Dave Howard Grain and Produce Co. of Bowling Green, Kentucky. Its partner was a Dorsey trailer. Notice the bug screen on the driver's left side mirror to keep the bugs from flying in the open window while driving. *Neil Sherff*

One of the many reefer carriers that ran up to the northeast from the southwest was Trans-Cold Express Inc. of Dallas, Texas. A lot of their loads to the northeast were Texas swinging beef carcasses. One of the many trucks they ran was this 4000 White with a Fruehauf reefer trailer. This tractor is dressed for road traveling. Notice all the license plates. Trans-Cold had a large fleet of owner operators. *Joe Wanchura*

Mayfair Industries Inc. manufactured windows, doors and window products. To haul their products to market they used a B-61 Mack with the integral sleeper cab and pulling a Fruehauf trailer. Mayfair Industries is from Lafayette, Louisiana. *Author Collection.*

A load of Duquesne beer was being hauled in this Fruehauf trailer. The A75T Autocar is pulling the trailer load of beer for the Golden Age Distributing Co. in Canton, Ohio. The power is from a 180-HP Cummins diesel engine with a 10-speed transmission and riding on 10:00-20 tires. *Autocar Trucks*

Interstate Dress Carriers were from New York City, New York. They operated a few different make of trucks in their fleet. One of those tractors was this GMC that pulled a Gindy trailer. Notice the Babaco Alarm Warning System signs on the trailers. *Author Collection*

The side-dump, bulk-hauling trailers were made for hauling oranges from the orange groves to the processing plant. The trailers are Utilities that are hooked to a nice looking G-73 Mack. The rig is owned by Earl P. Morse Trucking of Riverdale, California. *Utility Trailer Co.*

A company that ran coast to coast back in the early sixties was T.I.M.E. Freight Inc. in Lubbock, Texas. They ran in the southwest and on into the southern states. The tractor is a Model 5000 White and is pulling a 40-foot Fruehauf open-top trailer. In the later sixties Time Freight Inc. became part of the big Time DC operation. *Time Freight Inc.*

Spector Freight System Inc. of Chicago, Illinois ran double 40-foot trailers on both the Indiana and Ohio turnpikes as well as the New York State thruway and the Mass. turnpike. They covered an area from Texas up to the Great Lakes and on east into New England. This 9000 White and twin Fruehauf 40-foot trailers are running on the Ohio turnpike. At this point they are in the doubles hook up area. *Krohn Studios*

Nu Car Carriers in Metuchen, New Jersey was one of the many car haulers in the East. Many of their tractors were F-800 Fords and Troyler trailers. The cars they hauled were, of course, Fords. Five cars was the capacity on a rig like this one that hauled in the eastern states. *Neil Sherff*

Two reefer haulers were taking a break when this picture was taken. Both trucks are for Lake Refrigerated Service of Ridgefield, New Jersey. The one in view is a 923B Diamond T with a Trailmobile reefer trailer. The driver had the comfort of a sleeper box. *Neil Sherff*

Big job for big trucks. That was the order of the day when it was time to move the big heavy piece. The AP19 Autocar diesel had a 275-inch wheelbase riding on 14:00-24 tires. Power was a 430 HP diesel engine teamed with a 6-speed transmission. The truck was owned by the Arizona Public Service Co. in Farmington, New Mexico. *Autocar Trucks*

The Brockway Factory in Cortland, New York put out a lot of good, tough trucks. This Brockway Huskie is a good example. It sports a sleeper cab and is powered by a diesel engine. R.F. Edgecomb Trucking in Liberty, Maine is the owner. *Brockway Trucks*

This 990 Diamond T is a short BBC, (Bumber to back of cab), tractor. The company chose to add a sleeper box. It was pulling a 1950's Dorsey reefer trailer to deliver its load at a California dock. G+S Fruit Co. is the owner. *Stan Holtzman*

Another Mack is this B-73 that is powered by a Cummins diesel. It pulled a reefer trailer. This Mack has the "B" Series cab where a lot of the B-73's had the older "L" Series cab. The rig was leased on with Ewell Hodges of Denver, Colorado and Lakeland, Florida. Bullet cab-lights, dual stacks, sun visor, a sleeper box and trailer high stack make this a great looking truck. *Neil Sherff*

The new Mack "F" Series cab was introduced in 1962. It was available in two versions, a day cab and a sleeper cab as seen here. This is a Model F-611. It was owned by the Jim Bogetto Meat Co. Inc. of Tampa, Florida. It pulled a Fruehauf reefer trailer. *Harris Ray Photos*

This W-921 sits proud with a brand new set of bulk cement trailers. The Kenworth and the trailers make a nice outfit. The company is California based Bulk Transportation. *Author Collection*

In 1962, White-Freightliner built this experimental Conventional tractor. It was never put into production. It wasn't until ten years later that White-Freightliner made the first Conventional tractor in 1973. *Freightliner Corp.*

A lot of drivers had their own engineering designs of how they wanted their truck. This is a good example of that. Most drivers would have gotten a sleeper cab but this guy decided that he wanted to rest in peace on the second floor. The tractor he chose is a N-1000 Dodge to pull the Fruehauf moving-van trailer. The truck was for The Three Ivory Bros. in Centerline, Michigan who were agents for Allied Van Lines. The early "N" Series Dodges had the dual headlights: the singles came around 1967. *Neil Sherff*

The new 9000 White went through some changes. The big change was the new Autocar driver cab. Many companies liked the new change and its appearance. One of those companies was Branch Motor Express Co. in New York City, New York. This 9000 was hooked to a Gindy open-top trailer. *White Motor Co.*

Cooper-Jarrett Motor Freight Inc. of Chicago, Illinois was known as the route of the Relay Company. Cooper Jarrett had a lot of GMC tractors in their fleet like this 8000 Series that was hooked to a reefer trailer with two reefer units. On the back lot we can see some of their older tractors. Cooper Jarrett's operating area was from Kansas City to New York City with Relay stations in between. *United Press International*

The new D-400 Series in 1961 was available in several models. It was also known as the Emeryville because they used the Emeryville cab. This cab gave the drivers plenty of maneuvering room. The tractor is pulling a set of hopper-bottom, dump-trailers. *Bert Goldrath Photo*

This 921-F Diamond T was kept busy delivering gasoline in this Butler tank trailer for the Continental Oil Co. They advertise as the hottest brand going. *Hopkins Photography*

Another big refrigerated carrier was Frozen Food Express of Dallas, Texas. One of the rigs in their fleet was this DCO-405 International "Emeryville" that pulled a 40-foot Fruehauf reefer trailer. In their early years, their main operating territory was from Texas up to the Michigan and Chicago area and to the west coast. *Neil Sherff*

John Schutt Jr. Trucking Co. in Buffalo, New York was a bulk cement hauler. One of the trucks they used was this C-1000 Ford pulling a Fruehauf bulk cement-tanker 35- foot trailer. The tractor had a 135- inch wheelbase on 11x24.5 tires. The engine is a Ford 534 4v SD engine teamed with and Allison MT42 transmission. *Ford-Houston Branch*

At first glance you say that this is an International. Well, right and wrong. The cab is an International but it is really an 830-C Diamond T. It is a dump truck with a Spangler conversion. It is owned by John J. Jaro of Uniontown, Pennsylvania. As we can see it is a twin steering. *Author Collection*

Some companies were made up of owner-operator's equipment with just a few of their own. Diamond Transportation System in Racine, Wisconsin was one of those carriers. This GMC 7000 tractor that is powered by a V-6 GM engine is pulling a trailer load of cast pipes. A sleeper box was added along with dual stacks to dress it up a little bit. *Neil Sherff*

Although this photo was professionally taken, it is not quite clear enough to see what this model is. It could be a B53 mixer series for Mack. The brand name of the mixer body is also unknown. We do know that Tampa Sand and Material Co. in Tampa, Florida is the owner. Notice the high fenders with an added skirt. *Author Collection*

The big N-1000 Series Dodge was posing for the picture with its brand new partner, an American reefer trailer. They selected a sleeper box for those overnight or long distance runs. The Maxwell Seed and Produce Co. of North Little Rock, Arkansas is the owner. It is numbered unit 103. *American Trailer Co.*

This Kenworth truck-trailer tanker pulls up to get loaded with gasoline to make the day's delivery. The delivery source is Gasoline Tank Service Co. in Bellevue, Washington. *Author Collection*

This 1962 White-Freightliner is sitting here as a brand new truck. The dromedary body and trailer are both Utility. The colors are the colors of Grarrison Fast Freight Inc. which Consolidated Freightways Inc. purchased in 1957. The trucks are the Alaska division of C.F. the Dromedary body can be removed from the chassis. Bobbi Felix White-Freightliner

T.J. Dodd Trucking in Visalia, California is the owner of this DCO-405 International "Emeryville" that is pulling a set of bottom-unload, bulk-tank-trailers. The brand name is unknown. The company decided to go with the 80-inch sleeper cab. *Author Collection*

The Michigan Milk Producers Association in Detroit, Michigan decided to go with this HD-1000 Ford to pull the two milk-tanker trailers of unknown brand. The tractor rides on a 134- inch wheelbase on 10:00x20 tires. The power comes from a NH-220 Cummins diesel hooked up with an R-96 10-speed transmission. The average was 6.1 mpg grossing 97,000 lbs. M.M.P.A. had 6 of these units. *Ford Branch-Houston*

The Michigan steel haulers liked their many axles. The 3-3-3-3-1 set up is pulled by a 1000 Model Dodge cab-over-engine tractor. Capitol Transportation Co. owned the rig. After a few years the axles decreased to 12, then 11 and then to 10 or less. Both trailers are Fruehaufs. *Dodge Truck News*

Prouty Trucking in Pomona, California had this Model 35/ Peterbilt cab-over-engine pulling a set of bottom dump bulk-trailers of an unknown brand. Many unusual looking trailers could be seen throughout the western states. *Brian Williams*

Little Audreys Transportation Co. in Fremont, Nebraska was a big reefer hauler from Chicago to the west coast. A variety of different makes of tractors made up the fleet. Here we have a 931-C Diamond T pulling a Fruehauf reefer trailer. Frozen meats and meat by-products from Illinois, Iowa and Nebraska and Wisconsin cheese were some of the commodities they hauled to the west coast. *Neil Sherff*

The unbranded rig sitting here is a DLR 8000 GMC hooked up to a Fruehauf trailer. This is supposedly a smooth riding tractor because of air ride. Notice that the truck parked aside of this one is also a DLR 8000 GMC for Derosa Transportation Co. of Chicago, Illinois. *Neil Sherff*

The D-400 International was available in several versions of long nose, short nose, axle forward, axle back, tandem axle, single axle, day cab and sleeper cab like the one seen here. The Emeryville cab was used on this D-400 Series. Both Cummins and Detroit diesels were offered and an IHC 817 turbo charged was offered. *Author Collection*

Kenworths were a very popular truck in the state of Texas. Here were see two Kenworth cab-over-engine tractors, one pulling a Brown reefer trailer and the other a Fruehauf combination livestock and reefer trailer. Other trucks are leased to the A.T.A. of Texas (Agricultural Transportation Association of Texas) marketing Co-op. The company was started by Jack Cobb. *Skeet Richardson Photos*

Walnut Grove Products in Atlantic, Iowa purchased 14 Model HDT-950 tractors like the one we see here. They had a 158-inch wheelbase riding on 10:00x20 tires. NH 220 HP Cummins diesels supplied the power matched up to a Fuller RA-96 10-speed transmission. The trailer is a Fruehauf. They hauled payloads of 46,0000 pounds and grossed 71,600 pounds. The trailer was 35-feet long. *Ford-Houston Branch*

When you see this D-9000 GMC with the two big tanker-trailers and all the axles, you would think that this tractor has its hands full. There is a lot of weight there but it is probably equipped with a 8V-71 Detroit diesel putting out 318 HP. It pulls everything behind it with ease on the 3-2-3-2-1 axle set up. The two trailers are Fruehaufs. The rig belongs to the Shell Oil Co. in Detroit, Michigan. *Author Collection*

This N-1000-D Ford is one of two that are owned by Food Haul Inc. of Columbus, Ohio. It has a 146- inch wheelbase with a Fuller R-96 10 speed direct transmission riding on 10:00x20 tires. The engine is a Cummins NHE-195. The trailer is a Fruehauf. *Ford-Houston Branch*

A.B. Woodall Trucking took to the road with a set of bulk, tank-trailers. This California- based company is using a 931-F Diamond T to do the job. The 931 had the higher radiator over the other Diamond T models. *Author Collection*

This White-Freightliner was kept busy puling the Brown reefer trailer. It was employed by Colonial and Pacific Frigidway Inc. of Storm Lake, Iowa. This tractor is wearing all the chrome jewelry that made it a real nice looking tractor. The company had some nice looking tractors running for them in their fleet. *Neil Sherff*

Here again is one of two F-950 Ford tractors. They were owned by Merchants Trucking Co. of Norfolk, Virginia. The power was a Ford 477-4V-5.0 engine riding on 10:00x20 tires. Everything rode on a 146-inch wheelbase. The trailer is a Fruehauf flatbed. Steel is the load on this run. *Houston Branch*

Here is another Michigan-type gasoline hauling train. The tank trailers are Fruehaufs. The 3-2-3-2-1 rig is owned by A+C Carriers Inc. in Muskegon, Michigan. The tractor is a K-100 Kenworth. *A. Schultz Photo*

The blue and white tractors of The Middle Atlantic Transportation Co. Inc. of New Britain, Conn. could be seen traveling on the highways between New England and Michigan. A variety of different tractors made up the fleet. Here we have a D-9000 GMC with a Trailmobile van -trailer. In the later sixties Middle Atlantic was purchased by Branch Motor Express Inc. of New York City, New York. *Neil Sherff*

The C- Line became reality in 1963. Shown here is a C-600 model Mack that had an 89- inch BBC. The engine in this one is the end 864-V8. It had swing out fenders for easy access for maintenance. It could also pull a 40-foot trailer legally. *Mack Trucks*

Here is a C-600 at work. It is pulling a flatbed-trailer loaded with concrete castings. These were being delivery to somewhere in the Pennsauken, New Jersey area. The date was March 20, 1964. *Robert Parrish*

Peters Bros Inc. in Lenhartsville, Pennsylvania got their start in 1952 with a 650 GMC. They started hauling livestock from the Midwest stockyards into the east coast. They did this into the eighties. They have since gone out of livestock hauling and are now into reefer hauling. Their fleet of reefers is now over 60 rigs. The also have a terminal in Jerffersonville, Wisconsin. The truck seen here is a 352 Peterbilt with a Wilson livestock-trailer. All their trucks were show pieces and still are today. *Ron Adams*

This "S" Series Kenworth was introduced in 1961. However this photo was taken in 1964. The Socony Mobil Oil Co. in Minnesota owns the rig. The gasoline tank-trailer stretches out to 40 feet. *Author Collection*

This 7000 Model GMC was owned by C+M Trucking in Norwalk, California. It is set up as a transfer dump. It had a 6V-71 Detroit diesel engine. These transfer dumps were popular in the west. *Author Collection*

No, Billy the Kid is not the driver. That is just the brand name of the slacks that are loaded in the trailer. The tractor is a DCOF-405 International "Emeryville" with the 80-inch cab. The trailer is a Trailmobile. The owner is Hortex Manufacturing Co. of El Paso, Texas. *Author Collection*

The New York state thruway had many doubles like this. In this case there are two milk tanker-trailers that are hooked to a White 7000 that is owned by C+E Trucking Co. of Saugerties, New York. Both tank-trailers were made by Heil. *Author Collection*

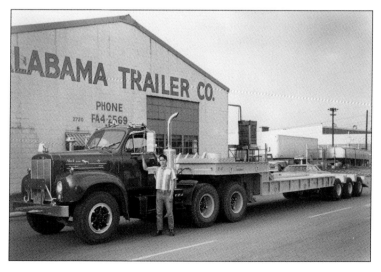

The driver stands real proud aside the truck that he is driving. It is a B-615 Mack that has the big end 864 diesel engine in it. It hosts dual chrome stacks, air cleaner, grille guard, and home number. The trailer is an Alabama drop deck. *Ken Ives Studio/ Alabama Trailer Co.*

Montgomery Ward stores had this White-Freightliner Tractor pulling a set of Utility double trailers. The tractor matches nice with the new set of doubles. *Author Collection*

One of the trucking companies that left the trucking scene 35 years ago was Navajo Freight Line Inc. in Denver, Colorado. It was sold to Arkansas Best Freight (ABF). In the mid- sixties this was one of the trucks they were operating in the west. It is a DCOF-405 International "Emeryville". The twin trailers are Trailmobiles. Many of us remember this name. *Navajo Freight Lines Inc.*

Here we have a real great looking F-700 Mack with an outside frame flatbed trailer. The rig is owned by WM. J. Winter Hay and Grain of Arlington, Nevada. A lot of chrome items give this tractor a very nice appearance. *Neil Sherff*

This setting in front of the Florida palm trees is a great backdrop for the Tropicana shot. Orange juice is the load headed for America's grocery stores. A D-9000 Series GMC is teamed up with a Trailmobile reefer trailer for the transportation of the product. A Thermo-King reefer unit keeps the load at controlled cold temperatures. Tropicana Products resides in Bradenton, Florida. *Lamar Philpod Photo*

C+H Transportation Co. of Dallas, Texas was a heavy-hauler carrier. Machinery, steel products, military equipment, oilfield equipment and cast pipes, like the load we see here, were some of the heavy-haul commodities that C+H transported. A lot of their runs were long runs or coast-to-coast runs. Owner operators made up a large part of their fleet. One of those rigs is this H-950 Ford with a flatbed-trailer hauling a load of cast pipes. The driver could have been from Mt.Pleasant, Texas. *Joe Wanchura*

An International Fleetstar 2000 diesel serves as the power source pulling a Trailmobile open-top trailer for J.W. Ward Trucking Co. of Murphysboro, Illinois. The Fleetstar was one of several different Star models that International offered. *J.W. Ward Trucking*

Many reefer haulers were located in the midwestern states. Some ran to the east coast and some ran to the west coast. Rowley Interstate Inc. of Dubuque, Iowa was one of the companies that ran out of Iowa to the east coast. This load was hauled by a K-100 Kenworth and a Brown reefer trailer. Rowley had a lot of fancied up tractors running in their fleet. Notice that at one time this trailer belonged to Frozen Food Express Inc. of Dallas, Texas. *Neil Sherff*

The western states saw many long-wheelbase tractors running their highways. Not only trucking companies ran them but also some private carriers. One of those private carriers was Georgia-Pacific Corp. out of Tigard, Oregon. This White-Freightliner, fancied up, has a Dromedary body and is pulling a Utility trailer. An air conditioner, 4 air horns, 5 bullet lights, dual spot lights, 4 road lights, and chrome front wheels are some of the added extras. *Neil Sherff*

This Oklahoma-based rig is a C-800 Ford. It was fitted with an open-rack side-body and a matching body to go with it. The truck is owned by the Phillips 66 Oil Co. in Bartelsville, Oklahoma. A real cool looking outfit. *Phillips 66 Oil Co.*

Back in the sixties is when Kenworth really started coming up with the real fancy paint designs. This K-100 Kenworth is perfect example of that. Daugherty Trucking in Findley, Ohio was the owner of the rig but it was leased on with Propane Transport Inc. in Milford, Ohio. The propane tank-trailer is of an unknown brand. *Neil Sherff*

The northwest was a big lumber hauling area. Here we see an F-700 Mack Western as a tri-axle with a flatbed trailer behind. The Pack River Company in Coeur D'Alene, Idaho is the company hauling the load of lumber. *Author Collection*

Caddell Transit Corp. of Lawton Oklahoma teamed up with this tanker-trailer to haul asphalt. The tractor is a Model 7000 White. A lot of tank- trailers were designed to haul certain liquid commodities. *Ray Jacoby Photography*

Back in the sixties, triple-trailers were being experimented with in the west. After some experimenting they were finally legalized. One of the companies benefitting this was Pacific Intermountain Express (P.I.E.) of Oakland, California. A Model 282 Peterbilt is pulling a train of three Trailmobile trailers. *P.I.E.*

V-J Derstine in Hatfield, Pennsylvania ran a fleet of livestock trucks between the East and Chicago. This green and white W-900 Kenworth and Fruehauf livestock-trailer were caught at the Chicago stockyards loading hogs. They were shipped to the Hatfield Packing Co. in Hatfield, PA. *Neil Sherff*

This big H-950 Ford diesel and Fruehauf reefer trailer were taking a break from their driving time. Morgan McCool Fruit Products Co. was based in Traverse City, Michigan. The big Ford has a sleeper cab. *Neil Sherff*

This Michigan gravel rig has a 3-2-4-2-1 axle configuration, 44 tires in all. The tractor is a 400 Series Brockway. Holloway Sand and Gravel Trucking Co. in Wixon, Michigan is the owner. When loaded, the GVW was well over 100,000 pounds. *Neil Sherff*

This is a 1966 W-900 Kenworth that was owned by Dan Calverly who lived in Ben Wheeler, Texas when he was not out on the road. He had tractor 521 leased on with C+H Transportation Co. of Dallas, Texas. On this trip he was hauling an under-cover load. The picture was taken at Mike + Vic's truck stop in North Lima, Ohio. *Robert Parrish*

This 1966 Model 352 Peterbilt was owned by Jim Haggard of Bell, California. A Highway trailer hauls his refrigerated cargo. He has this as tractor number one. It looks like he has a plan to add more tractors. *Robert Parrish*

By this time, Diamond T got away from the louvers on the side of the hood and went to the flat side with the Diamond T emblem. This 923-B was owned by the Stone Container Corp. based in Ohio. It got matched up with a Fruehauf trailer with spread axles. *Neil Sherff*

The Convoy Company in Portland, Oregon had a fleet of various types of configurations for hauling cars. This 1000 Series Dodge tractor hauls four cars and seven on the trailer. This was the western type of car transporter compared to our four and five type car hauler in the east. *Ackroyd Photography*

This photo that was taken in 1968 off the turnpike at the Carlisle, Pennsylvania exit. The building in the background is the old Flemmings truck stop which closed in 1969. The truck in action is a CO-4000 International pulling a Fruehauf trailer. The company is Navajo Freight Lines Inc. of Denver, Colorado. It shows a new tractor with the old graphics on the trailer. *Ron Adams*

Humble Oil and Refining Company had a nationwide fleet of trucks. This is one of the trucks in their western fleet. It is a Model 351 Peterbilt with a tank-body and a pull-trailer behind. A Cummins diesel is most likely the power source. *Humble Oil and Refining Co.*

The Continental Conveyor and Equipment Co. of Winfield, Alabama decided to use a CO-4000 International for hauling their products on the flatbed trailer. Notice the position of the loads to balance out the weight on the trailer tandem, tractor tandem and the steering axle. *Author Collection*

As we know, the south was a big agricultural part of our country. Fruits and produce had to be shipped to markets. One of those haulers and shippers was Alterman Transport Lines in Miami, Florida. One of the rigs they used was a W-1000 Ford with a Great Dane reefer trailer. Their shipping area was up into the Midwest and the Northeast. *Harry Patterson*

George Transfer and Rigging Co. Inc. of Baltimore, Maryland was also a steel hauler, although the Brown van-trailer hooked to the Diamond T tractor is not a flat bed like you would expect to see when mentioning steel hauling, it was probably used for handing special loads. *Neil Sherff*

A company that put on a good display of sharp looking equipment was International Transport Inc. of Rochester, Minnesota. This heavy-hauling carrier had a big variety of different brand names of trucks in their fleet. One of those trucks was this K-100 Kenworth. It was owned by owner-operator Ron Drayton. It was pulling a Brown open-top trailer with an under-cover load in it. They hauled a lot of farm implements, military equipment, steel products, plus other heavy equipment. *Harry Patterson*

The moving companies seemed to have a lot of sharp looking tractors in their fleets. This K-100 is a perfect example of that. Bekins Van Lines Inc. had this Kenworth running across the country moving people in style. *Harry Patterson*

On this long wheelbase RL-700 Mack it looks like they tried to squeeze every inch they could use for cargo. The body on the chassis was also probably used for hauling grain. I do not know the owner or the truck's home location, but you can tell it is from somewhere in the western states. *Harry Patterson*

Lets title this picture "The Volume Hauler for Lite Weight Freight." The K-100 Kenworth with it's 48-inch cab also used all the extra space they could on the long-wheelbase tractor. The dromedary body and trailer were both made by Utility. Notice the doors on the front of the trailer. The purpose of this is probably to unload the trailer first and then the freight in the body could be unloaded through the trailer. Guthmiller Trucking Inc. of Lodi and Oakland, California were the owners. *Author Collection*

This western-type, truck-trailer combination is hauling an under-cover load on a flat-bed trailer. Everything is on the chassis of a White-Freightliner. Truck number 40 is owned by Mellow Equipment Co. Inc. which is probably an Oregon-based carrier. *Author Collection*

This W-1000 Ford is taking a break from it all. The rig is owned by A. Brandt Co. of Fort Worth, Texas. They are manufacturers of "Ranch Oak" furniture. *Harry Patterson*

Another K-100 Kenworth is taking time out from a long, hard up-grade pull for cooling down. A dromedary body and a Utility reefer trailer are hauling the load "Thirst Quencher" compliments of the Olympia Brewing Co. The beer kegs in the body are mostly empty while the cool stuff is in the trailer. Santry Trucking Co. in Portland, Oregon is the hauler. *Brian Williams*

Kaiser Aluminum, Chemicals and Refactories in Oakland, California operates this White-Freightliner and Fruehauf coverta-flat trailer with removable sides. The rig is on lease from Ryder truck rentals. *Author Collection*

From the big sky country we have the Union Tractor Co. of Dillon, Montana. They owned the tractor which is a W-900 Kenworth. In 1969 they leased their trucks on with the Big Sky Farmers and Ranchers Marketing Co-Op of Montana with offices in Great Falls, Montana and Artesia, California. They hauled agricultural produce and shrubbery nationwide. The tractor was sold through the Motor Power Equipment Co. in Billings, Montana who was the Kenworth dealer. This tractor is pulling a Fruehauf reefer trailer. *Harry Patterson*

Pick-N-Pay got their goods delivered in this Timpte reefer trailer. A White 4000 is the tractor pulling the trailer. The driver sits in the Autocar cab that White was using at the time. Cargo in the trailer was kept cool by a Thermo-King reefer unit. *Timpte Trailers*

A truck-trailer combination for a private carrier. This short nose 9500 GMC is the truck with a Utility truck body and a Utility trailer. Sexton Quality Foods is the owner of the rig. Some private carriers also used these truck-trailer combinations. *Author Collection*

By this time, Reo and Diamond T were merged into one company and then became Diamond-Reo in 1967. This Diamond Reo is an example of that joint venture. The trailers are aluminum doubles used to haul cement and other powdered materials. Capacity is 1100 cubic feet. Butler is the brand name of the trailer. *Butler Tank + MFG. Co.*

Another carrier from the South is Greenstein Trucking Co. of Pompano Beach, Florida. They also hauled southern fruit and produce to the Midwestern states and also up to the northeast. On this trip we see tractor number 93, a K-100 Kenworth, pulling a Great Dane stainless steel reefer trailer. The green, black, white and gold stand out with all the chrome bells and whistles. *Neil Sherff*

Willis Shaw Frozen Express Inc. in Elm Springs, Arkansas had a large fleet of trucks that consisted of Kenworth and White-Freightliner Trucks. They did however have a few lease operators running with their fleet. An example of one is the model 359 Peterbilt pulling one of Shaw's Trailmobile reefer trailers. Check out those dual trailer high stacks. *Harry Patterson*

Rox Bros. Inc. of Tucson, Arizona owned this 1969 Diamond Reo that pulled a flatbed trailer with screened insides. It looks like lumber could be the cargo inside the fence. Notice that nice Arizona scenery in the background. *Gene Wendt Tucson Diesel Inc.*

In 1970 Ford came out with their new "L" Series known as the Louisville Ford. The one seen here is the L-9000. Caterpillar, Cummins and Detroit diesels were offered as the power sources. Ford gasoline engines were also offered. These trucks were made at Ford's plant in Louisville, Kentucky which is where it got the name "Louisville" Ford. It was the largest truck plant in the world. They could produce 336 units per day on three parallel assembly lines. They turned out to be very popular trucks. Ford Motor Co.

The Adams World Wide Movers from New Jersey is family owned and operated since 1872. The moving specialist used this Diamond Reo tractor and moving-van trailer to perform their services. *Author Collection*

During the sixties a lot of the truck manufacturers made a lot of changes in the design of their trucks and GMC was no exception. The previous cracker-box cab was more of a box type cab. The Astro 95 had more rounded corners and a bigger windshield along with different type mirrors. New paint designs and color schemes came along with the package. *GMC Trucks*

When you were hauling livestock the routine was get them loaded and get them there in short order. Brad Dufy from California intended to do just that with his White-Freightliner and his set of Merritt livestock-trailers. The tractor has many chrome extras and gives it a nice appearance, especially the double chrome numbers. *Brian Williams*

The Northwest is known for lumber cutting and finishing. From the process of trimming down logs, you get a lot of wood chips. These wood chips needed to be taken to a processing plant. This W-900 Kenworth and the Peerless wood chip hauling trailer are there to do just that. *Author Collection*

The Model 359 Peterbilts made a big hit with owner operators and small fleet operators. Here we see one that is owned by Ken Lowry. He is pulling a Trailmobile reefer trailer. The picture was taken in 1972 at the Bartonsville 76 truck stop in Bartonsville, Pa. *Harry Patterson*

Driver Joel Willis gives us a friendly wave as he and the GMC Astro 95 and Great Dane trailer pose for the photo shoot. Parramore and Griffin was the company. They went by the name Pee-Gee Chemicals in Valdosta, Georgia. *Author Collection*

A brand new stainless steel milk tanker body sits on the chassis of this new Model 358 Brockway straight truck. Owner Mort Robertson of Richfield Springs, New York makes his farm- to-farm rounds picking up milk for shipment to the dairies. This Brockway is one of the 8 trucks in the fleet. Brockway Trucks

In the late sixties and early seventies Brockway came out with a line of new models. Here we see a 359 TL hooked to a Trailmobile open, rack side, flatbed trailer. Craine Inc. of Barneveld, New York was the owner of the rig. They manufactured silos and feeding systems. The names of the two gentlemen are not known. Brockway Trucks

Consolidated Freightways Inc. of Menco Park, California had several divisions in their operation. One of those was a tanker hauling operation that covered the western states. One of the rigs used was this White-Freightliner truck-trailer-tanker outfit used for hauling gasoline. *Author Collection*

A member of the Transtar family was this International DCF-400. These were available in both the long hood and short hood. As for power, they could get an in-line six, V6, V8 by International, Cummins or Detroit diesel. The rig was with the Murphy-Miles Div. for the Amaco Oil Company in Chicago, Illinois. *Author Collection*

Another set of doubles is this Peterbilt Model 359 with a set of American bottom-hopper, grain-trailers. The rig operated out of Brush, Colorado. Notice that the license plates are still a part of the trucking dress code at this time. *Harry Patterson*

Another grain hauler is this long nose 9500 Series GMC pulling a Timpte bottom-dump, grain-trailer. I don't know who the owner was but who ever it was certainly did a nice job of his selection of the color scheme and design. *Harry Patterson*

Another type of Michigan doubles is this set of milk tankers that are being pulled by a GMC Astro tractor. The trailer is a Progress Model MTT-RD 12,000 gallon train. The tractor has a 150-inch wheelbase. The owner is Edmund Snaden of Hudsonville, Michigan and has the tractor leased on with Milk Transport. *Progress Industries*

Construction Haulers Inc. of Grand Rapids, Michigan was one of the many gravel haulers in the state. A lot of them were gravel trains like this one. Kenworth tractors were a popular brand with the drivers along with the Fruehauf twin dump-trailers. They had various axle configurations like this 3-2-2-2-1. Notice the sturdy frame on the trailers. All those axles means a lot of payload. *Neil Sherff*

Fresh off the line is this Model 360 Brockway, which is the axle forward version. The Huskie feels proud to be among all the shiny chrome options that are displayed on this 360. General Power Jet tires were selected to run on. *Brockway Trucks*

From Huskietown we have another Brockway. This time is a Model 361, which is the axle back version. Again, the Huskie feels proud to be displayed among all the shiny chrome. This one is powered by a Caterpillar diesel. *Brockway Trucks*

Eight-foot logs make up the load on this Oerecht flatbed trailer with seven axles. On the front end we have a K-100 Kenworth. Notice that the two front axles are air lifted off the pavement of the trailer. *Neil Sherff*

The Campbell Chain Co. is a division of Unitec Industries in York, PA, West Burlington, Iowa and Union City, California. One of the trucks in the fleet is the F-700 Mack used to pull the Gindy trailer. This one was home-based at the York, PA plant. *Jim Hayman Photography*

Back in the sixties and seventies there were a number of farm co-ops. Each one had their own fleet of trucks. American Farm Lines based in Oklahoma City, Oklahoma had their own fleet. One of the trucks was the Diamond Reo hooked up to a Hobbs trailer. Many of these Diamond Reos that had sleeper boxes usually had the stacks coming up behind the sleeper box. *Neil Sherff*

The western truck-trailer combinations could be seen with any type of body and pull trailer. In this case we have a propane body and trailer on a White-Freightliner truck. The makers of the body and trailer are unknown. Van Gas Inc. in Fresno, California is the owner of the rig. *Author Collection*

While driving down the road, trucks like this 352 Peterbilt Pacemaker really caught your attention. Al Clemons was the owner and had it leased on in the reefer division for Trans American Freight Lines Inc. of Detroit, Michigan. The trailer was a Gindy reefer. The tractor is a 1972 model. *Harry Patterson*

This time we have a set of double trailers. On the front end is a 282 Peterbilt pulling the Dorsey doubles. The rig belongs to the General Electric aircraft engine group in Cincinnati, Ohio. *Author Collection*

One of the biggest companies back in the day was Spector Freight System Inc. of Chicago, Illinois. All different types of equipment were used to cover the territory from Texas, Oklahoma, and Kansas all the way to New England. One of the rigs used was this GMC Astro 95 to pull the set of Monon trailers. Spector got its start back in 1930-31. *Spector Freight System*

Huskietown in the lights again with their new Model 761 Brockway in the axle back version. Caterpillar, Cummins and Detroit diesels were offered. A somewhat different paint scheme, but nice. *Brockway Trucks*

Another star in the International lineup was the Paystar 5000. The Paystar 5000 was the line for mixers and dump trucks and tractor for dump trailers and low beds. Several engines were offered in the Paystar series. *International Harvester Co.*

This 359 Peterbilt was one of many that were set up as a truck-trailer combination to run the western states. The body and trailer were designed for hauling gasoline. Both body and trailer were made by Fruehauf. The only name we can see is Lerner. *Author Collection*

With the many big ranches in the big state of Texas raising cattle, that meant that there were a lot of slaughter houses butchering cattle. In turn, that meant that there was a lot of meat and swinging beef to haul.. One of the many carriers was Jay Lines Inc. out of Amarillo, Texas. This Kenworth with the big 108-inch cab with a Utility reefer trailer on behind. A lot of these Texas reefer haulers ran up into the Northeast. *Harry Patterson*

In late 1972, this new Fleetstar 2070A joined two other models, the 2000 and 2100 models. It was designed to handle the big diesel engines and to be both a highway tractor and construction truck. It could handle engines up to 335 HP in highway models and 270 HP for construction models. This tractor is pulling a brand new Fruehauf trailer. *International Harvester*

May Trucking Co. in Payette, Idaho was mainly a western states carrier, but eventually years later became a 48-state hauler. Back in the day, one of the trucks they used was this early-seventies International Transtar and outside-frame, flatbed trailer. A lot of operators liked this type of trailer. *Author Collection*

Another western carrier that operated as a farm co-op was Tillamook Growers Co-op with offices in Paramount, California and Portland, Oregon. This real nice, two-tone blue W-900 Kenworth and Utility reefer trailer was one of the trucks that made coast-to-coast runs for the co-op. The owner named his truck "Sittin Bull" *Harry Patterson*

The moving companies always had lots of nice, clean-looking trucks running for them. This 352 Peterbilt is a perfect example of that. The trailer it is pulling is a Kentucky moving-van, reefer trailer. These were used for hauling loads that required a controlled climate. The company is United Van Lines Inc. of St.Louis, Missouri. *Harry Patterson*

The main course is on the way. This load of steaks is being shipped in style in this W-900 Kenworth and Utility trailer. Notice that the sleeper box could be a 40-inch box. I love those high stacks. Mr. Steak in Denver, Colorado is the owner. *Neil Sherff*

This L-9000 Ford was one of many that were in the fleet of Ryder Truck Lines based in Jacksonville, Florida. The L-9000 Ford was one of almost 1,000 over-the-road tractors and the Trailmobile trailer is one of over 4,400 road trailers. Their city fleet consisted of 966 tractors and 517 trailers plus 714 straight, city trucks. This equipment was stationed in 145 terminals in 31 states. *Robert Parrish*

Loaded and Rollin' is what this White-Freightliner is up to. It is bringing along two Utility trailers behind him. Milne served five western states. Notice the curbside doors on the front trailer for loading or unloading. *Author Collection*

A brand new model 459TL Brockway just came off the line. It got a custom paint job along with some chrome. There was a choice of either a Caterpillar or Detroit Diesel. The only thing that is missing is the fifth wheel. *Brockway Trucks*

Turner Bros. Trucking Co. in Oklahoma City, Oklahoma transported this load of unknown cargo. The driver had his model 352 Peterbilt with the 110-inch cab leased to Turner Bros. to pull this flatbed load. The dressed up tractor makes a good impression for the company. *Harry Patterson*

Sternlite Transportation Co. Inc. of Winsted, Minnesota had this 352 Peterbilt delivering nationwide. A dromedary body was added to handle extra cargo. Drivers say that the money earned from the freight on the dromedary pays for the truck's expenses and the money earned from the freight in the trailer is money in the bank. *Harry Patterson*

In 1973, White-Freightliner came out with their new Power Liner model. Bigger engines could be installed which is the reason for the larger grille. More airflow intake was required for cooling the high horsepower engines. *White- Freightliner*

The new International Transtar II was introduced in 1973. It was similar to the regular Transtar, but the cab was raised 5 inches to accommodate larger engines, including International's own 798 cu. in. V-800. The Tran star II did lose some weight verses the Transtar by using aluminum components. A Cummins NTC-290 was the standard engine. This single axle version is hauling two loads of straw. *Author Collection*

A Model 761 Brockway stands tall hooked up to the flatbed trailer. Like many of Brockway models; a Caterpillar, Detroit Diesel or Cummins diesel were offered. The big front end makes the Huskie look like he is ready to fight his way down the highway. It looks like a dump body is being shipped. *Brockway Trucks*

While it is time to take a driving break, this White-Freightliner and its trailer sits and waits for its driver to return and get back on the road again. The dromedary body is stacked with skids, which a lot of drivers had as extras. The rig was on with PTS Transportation Specialists Inc. of Portland, Oregon. *Author Collection*

The Diamond Reo Raider was introduced around 1974. Here we see another big grille tractor, which seemed to be the thing at the time. A new paint design was also introduced in several different color schemes. The Raider is pulling a Brown reefer trailer. The rig is leased on with Frostways Inc. of Detroit, Michigan. *Harry Patterson*

This truck needs no introduction. We all know who this is. It's Roadway Express Inc. of Akron, Ohio. The company got its start back in 1930 by two brothers, Carroll and Galen Roush. One tractor-trailer started it all. At this time Roadway was running several thousand tractors. One of them was this White Road Boss. Several other makes helped to make up the fleet. At this time they were the second or third largest carrier. *Roadway Express Inc.*

Another one of the larger carriers was Transcon Lines of El Segundo, California. Their fleet consisted of almost all White-Freightliners as seen here. Their tractor fleet totaled over 800 tractors. The trailer fleet totaled over 2,600 of various types and sizes. The set of doubles seen here were made by Strick. *Transcon Lines*

The "R" Model Mack was a popular truck with a lot of carriers. The R-600 Model we see here is owned by Penn Dixie Cement Corp. in Nazareth, Pennsylvania. It was used to pull the bulk-cement, tank-trailer. *Author Collection*

Marmon Trucks were good trucks, but they never seemed to be a real big hit like the other makes, but they got the job done just as well. This Marmon was leased on with McNamara Motor Express Inc. of Kalamazoo, Michigan. The seven-axle, flatbed-trailer was made by Delta. Cummins, Caterpillar, and Detroit diesel engines were offered. You could also get all the chrome bells-and-whistles as other trucks, as seen here. *Neil Sherff*

Kenworth was the first to have the high-rise cab known as the VIT 200 Aerodyne. There was plenty of room to stretch out in this cab. Mark Hill Haulers in Cullman, Alabama was the owner and pulled a Utility reefer trailer. *Harry Patterson*

Jones Motor Co. of Spring City, Pennsylvania was another one of the larger carriers. Their tractor fleet numbered over 950 and the trailers numbered 1,900 of various types. The tractor seen here is an L-9000 Ford with a dressed-up, van-trailer. *Jones Motor Co.*

Yellow Freight System in Shawnee Mission, Kansas covered almost every state in the United States.. One of their rigs was this GMC tractor and van-trailer. Back at this time some carriers had cut-off bumber. The reason for this was so the bumber wouldn't cut into the tires if there was an accident. *Yellow Freight System*

Here we have another case of the cut-off bumber. The R Model Mack and the Pines trailer was in the fleet of 316 tractors and 550 road trailers for Mushroom Transportation Co. in Philadelphia, Pennsylvania. They served seven Middle Atlantic states. *George Cleves*

The Ford W-9000 got a little bit of a new look with a grille change in the later seventies. The owner leased his tractor to North American Van Lines of Fort Wayne, Indiana. He pulled one of their Kentucky moving van trailers. *Harry Patterson*

In 1976, the agreement between the White Motor Co. and Freightliner Corp. expired. The name then went back to Freightliner. What we see here is a Freightliner truck-trailer combination as a flatbed. It looks like the load could be some kind of concrete product. *Author Collection*

The Conventional also went back to the name Freightliner. This tractor was hooked up to a reefer trailer. The rig was leased on the Altruk Freight System in Palo Alto, California. The color scheme and design was a very popular Freightliner design. It looks real good. *Author Collection*

Here we have another Ford W-9000, but this time as a tandem axle. The Globe-Union of Middletown, Delaware owned the truck. The photo was taken at the Peter Pan Diner in Kuhnsville, Pennsylvania *Ron Adams*

In 1978, Mack introduced their new Superliner. Its good looks put it right up with the rest of the other makers. The chrome and polished aluminum give it the custom look. The owner Barry Groff of York, Pennsylvania feels proud of this truck that is pulling a Timpte spread-axle, reefer trailer. *Neil Sherff*

Allied Van Lines Inc. of Broadview, Illinois always had sharp looking equipment in their fleet. An example of that is this Freightliner VanLiner that had the 104-inch cab. A dromedary body filled up the vacant space between the cab and the Kentucky trailer. Sometimes these bodies were made as living quarters but in this case it is a freight body. *Harry Patterson*

The Midwestern states had a lot of reefer haulers operating out of that area. One of those carriers was Holiday Express Inc. of Esterville, Iowa. They had a good number of nice looking trucks running for them, like this W-900 Kenworth with a Timpte reefer trailer. This paint scheme is similar to the one that Freightliner has. *Harry Patterson*

This "R' Model Mack got itself a three-color paint scheme. Drivers got their trucks painted up to their color and designed to their liking. M.B. Transport Inc. of Jamison, Pennsylvania employed this operator. The chrome moon hubcaps add a little more shine to the truck. *Harry Patterson*

This Western Star and Utility reefer trailer must be brand new because there is no name and no markings on it, but plenty of chrome. The Western Star started out as White Western Star in 1968. *Neil Sherff*

Monfort was known for their fast Kenworth trucks and the eye-catching color scheme of orange, yellow and white. This Freightliner tractor has the same design, but the colors are brown, cream and white. Monfort of Colorado was from Greeley, Colorado. I notice on the door that it says Steinbecker Bros. It is possible the Steinbecker Bros. could own the truck. A Timpte reefer trailer is the partner to the tractor. *Harry Patterson*

A truck-trailer combination with an Alloy, high-cube body and trailer. A Freightliner does the job of hauling the freight for Gordon Trucking Inc. of Tacoma, Washington. Aside of this rig is a Freightliner probably pulling a set of high-cube double trailers. *Author Collection*

The Model 359 Peterbilt was a very popular truck with owner operators. They had plenty of chrome and a lot of drivers chose a color scheme and design according to their taste. This one was hooked up with a Fruehauf reefer trailer. J+B Leasing Inc. of Toledo, Ohio was the owner. *Neil Sherff*

A Mack tractor has the honor of pulling a set of Monon double trailers down the highway for Advance-United Expressways in Minneapolis, Minnesota. The rig was known as the City of Council Bluffs. *Author Collection*

As we ride into the new decade of the eighties we remember that the trucks started to become more aero-dynamic. This model 377 Peterbilt started production in 1986. The 377 came with a 3406B Caterpillar engine with 310 HP as a standard engine. Optional engines were Caterpillar up to 425 HP or a Cummins Diesel from 300 up to 444 HP A+D Hitchcock Trucking Inc. of Webberville, Michigan were the proud owners of this 377 along with two Dorsey double-dump trailers. *Neil Sherff*

WOW. Take a look at this! Is there any room for anything else on this truck? Check out the chrome. Check out the mural. Check out all the lights. Check it all out. This Model 362 Peterbilt belongs to an owner operator in Ontario, Canada. The tractor has the 110-inch cab with an Aero-Dyne type sleeper on the back. The truck is known as "First Class". *Neil Sherff*